Poems from my window

A poetic journey

Joy Chippindale

© Joy Chippindale 2025

Illustrations: Holly Chippindale

Publishing partner: Paragon Publishing, Rothersthorpe

The rights of Joy Chippindale to be identified as the author of this work have been asserted by her in accordance with the Copyright, Designs and Patents Act of 1988.

All rights reserved; no part of this publication may be reproduced, stored in a retrieval system, or transmitted in any form or by any means, electronic, mechanical, photocopying, recording or otherwise without the prior written consent of the publisher or a licence permitting copying in the UK issued by the Copyright Licensing Agency Ltd. www.cla.co.uk

ISBN 978-1-78792-083-5

Book design, layout and production management by Into Print
www.intoprint.net

+44 (0)1604 832149

For Simon

Contents

Tree 7
You 9
Silence 13
Rain 15
Time 17
Little bird 19
Peanut 21
Book 24
Sheep 26
Kitty 29

Foreword

In early 2022, my Mum had a devastating fall that broke her hip, three ribs, sternum and multiple bones in her wrist, leaving her faced with a long and painful road to recovery. At the time, she had just been diagnosed with stage 4 osteoporosis, a condition that further complicated her healing process. Yet, despite the physical pain and emotional toll, she found a way to connect with her inner strength. As she sat for hours in quiet reflection, she began to write poems from her window.

What started as a means to express her deepest fears and struggles gradually became a source of healing and solace. Over the course of her recovery, she wrote poems that captured her journey. These ten selected poems published shift from the dark early days of recovery, to lighter ones as the healing progressed. The words are truly a testament to her resilience and openness to heal not only her body, but also her heart and mind.

It is with great pride and love that we share these poems with you, knowing that they carry not only Mums personal story of healing, but also a profound message of hope and strength for others facing their own challenges.

The decision to donate all proceeds from this book to Martin House Hospice is in memory of my Mum's cousin Paul.

Thank you for joining us in this journey, may these words touch your heart as they have touched ours.

Holly Chippindale

Tree

Earth is my food, within him I grow
My sacred roots wind deep and feast
My aged body, stoic, wise,
Why do you cry at your window?
I see you, I hear you,
and reach out in spirit
And dry your saddened eyes

Water is my life, I need it just like you,
And all that breathes on this earth
My aged body hydrated and cleansed,
Watch from your window as clouds release requisite rain,
Droplets so pure
And accept my prayers of gratitude,
you quench and you cure

Wind is my companion,
And with him I sing, and wave,
I sway and play,
My aged body, still, fluid, whole
Why don't you dance at your window?
I feel your pain, absorb it,
And heal your wretched soul

Fire is my nemesis,
And from him I hide,
In trepidation I avoid his destructive gaze.
My aged body will not surrender, depart
Please leave your window
Come speak to me,
Hug me
Your friend, Your tree, and allow me to heal your heart

You

A sudden fall, and all went dark
I searched my mind for you
Who are you? What are you?
Reveal and let me through

Racing mind, chaotic world
Took hold beyond control
I suffered the fall, yet felt release
From You who took its toll

And calm flowed through my broken bones
He spoke in quiet tongue
My eyes caught sight of life, of light
Not shone since I was young

For all we seek an endless climb
And fall to great accord
I wake to peace and pastures new
Rid life I'd long deplored

Envelop me in robes of silk and satin, smooth and strong,
Small steps of strength, of changing pace
A new world I now belong

And You, yes You
What, where, which, how you caged
An innocent child
You stole and gripped, but fall released
I leave you far behind

Warm sun, shines now through shorter nights
My moon lights longer days
Set free from chains of dread, despair,
those thoughts I have erased

You, take my hand, You
Weak, you're gone you're dead
You, hear my mind, feel my strength
Never rear your ugly head.

My bones are healed from painful fall
My scars remain unfound,
I'm all I've been, have learned and seen
I'm home on solid ground

And you, are gone, from earth, from me
And you, if, are, was, then, gone.
And you, however life unfolds, untold
Never, did You belong - goodbye You.

Silence

Is it ever truly silent
What is silence
Can I hear you call my name
playing on my conscious thought
telling tales, a teasing game

Are you really somewhere, silence
Where is silence
can I feel you touch my cheek
with gentle breath you linger
only I hear you speak

Show me what you are, silence
Who is silence
guide me to your hiding place
please tuck me under your blanket
and reveal your elusive face

I've caressed your presence, silence
Why are you silent
perpetually shrouded in your heavy cloak
stirring dormant emotions as I rise
a vision of hope you do evoke

Rain

Rain trickles down my window
and into my heart it sinks,
pressing grey into my already dull day,
I feel sad that you steal my last threads of contentment,
Oh cloud above, take your dreary burden away

Rain streams against my pane
and into my heart it seeps,
further deepening my already dark mood,
your tears sap energy from my core,
Oh cloud above, you are selfish, impatient, rude.

Rain hammers against my glass
and into my heart it weeps,
a veil of despair, I lower my blind,
icy thoughts channel my veins and poison my day,
Oh cloud above, you torment my troubled mind.

I try to sleep

Rays of sunshine flood my space
and into my heart they press,
bringing closure to my very long night,
I open my blind and your tears are gone,
Oh cloud above, you're gone - this new day is my beacon of hope and light.

Time

Tick tock, tick tock,
a painful noise, screaming at me, inside my head,
my cup empty, my heartbeat nowhere to be heard,
a piece of time, chiming misery and dread,
Chiming? -
A word which in time, I hold onto in hope,
as I spend endless hours alone, staring,
at beige walls in my beige world,
my pendulum now stopped, despairing,
In a case made of glass,
my hands stand stock still,
everyone else moving, living,
but not me, a broken element of time,
fragile, weak, pathetic, unforgiving.

Little bird

Little bird you've landed, I hear your call,
Astonishingly shrill for a creature so small,
As morn breaks through, you leave your nest,
and seek my wall, to think and rest.

Little bird, today I wait in earnest for you,
to bring me cheer for I feel blue,
my heart does glow to see your face,
your joyous dawn chorus I fondly embrace

Little bird, you stare at me,
your tiny, knowing eyes through which you see me,
a forlorn broken figure staring back,
energy and positivity, today I so lack.

Little bird, delicate and fragile yet incredibly strong,
Knowing and proud as you sing me your song,
of wisdom and hope, a thought calming tune,
I've missed you today, please come back soon.

Little bird, come share your story,
I yearn to hear it in all its glory,
and spread my wings and take my flight,
Please pass on your strength so I can battle this fight.

Little bird, you're my teacher of spiritual calm,
your friendship is soothing, a rich healing balm,
As springtime moves on, you perch earlier each morn,
Chirpy and bright, never cross or forlorn.

Little bird, could I ask of you, one day if I may,
to help carry my deep, heavy burdens away,
and though this may seem fundamentally absurd,
I'll grow imaginary wings and fly high with you, little bird.

Peanut

Small I may be, but challenge me not
I'm a tough little nut to crack
I'm the king of the herd, always have the last word
I'm Peanut, the man of the pack

Hardy and strong, long legged with horns
My barrel is stocky and deep
With a nose short and wide,
And my wiry brown hide
Boy can I rock a great leap!

Fussy with food? I'm not one to deny
My preference is fresh picked and green
Apple not pear
Feed me plums if you dare
I need to keep fit, lithe and lean

We pygmies are cute
But lest you forget
We have our off days just like you
And as head of my tribe, if you get my goat vibe,
At breakfast I'm first in the queue

Now Pixie my girlfriend, so pretty and trim
She's feisty, nimble and bright
She's risqué and fun,
As we frolic in the sun
Then we star gaze together by night

It's a goat's life you bet
Nothing better on earth
Climbing my tower so tall
Watching humans walk by, exclaiming,
"Oh my oh my
there's a goat over that dry stone wall!"

How rude people are - do they not understand
We goats need our privacy too
Our unique bulbous eyes, too often criticised
Ensure nothing stays far out of view

And oh can I shout and let it all out
No need for guard dogs with me
At night I do sleep, one ear open I keep,
To alert Nigel if need be, you see

I'm Peanut, I'm proud, to be chief goat on the farm
I'll allow you to pat my sweet head
I've told you my tale, now I'll munch on my kale
Then I'll retire to my cosy, snug bed

Book

Touching your cover, I judge you not
Illustration can't capture the power,
A deeply profound
Spiritual flight I embrace
A journey to change I devour

Reading - a reflection of my past
Of perfection I so desperately sought
Once void of direction
You took my hand
Enlightened my path to calm thought

Turning your pages, hurt and pain I have faced
Of how and why I became me
Arising from surfacing truths buried deep
Once blinded, but now I can see

I've read you, believe me, you'll never be closed
My compass, you showed me the end
A companion I treasure, no shelf shall you sit
My savior, my teacher, my friend.

Sheep

Beneath my ponderous coat of wool which defines me,
who, what am I?
Just a sheep, some might say, and so with a heavy sigh
Oh, how I yearn to…
Open up your static mind
Extend your stagnant view
I'm a wise, inventive, being
A gentle, innocent Ewe

I own a name, I feel pain
Have days when I feel blue
My friends I love, they love me back
We think, cry, laugh, like you
Oh how I yearn to…
Open up your blinkered eyes
Expunge your archaic view,
Eat what grows, not walks, nor talks
Not me, a harmless Ewe

In herd we roam our paddock green
As one we meditate
We search for calm, we fear the storm
And pray it will abate
Oh how I yearn to…
Open up your frozen heart
Respect us, as we do you
Deeply complex woolly jewels,
Me - a brilliant Ewe.

Kitty

Oh Kitty my darling, you fascinate me
Your actions are funny, they fill me with glee
In tough times you've been here from morning till night
Always around me, never far out of sight

Oh Kitty my sweet pea you never do cease,
To lighten my thoughts and bring my release
Of frustration, desire, to be up on my feet
Playing mousy and ball would be such a huge treat.

Oh Kitty my baby, your dense velvet fur
I could stroke you for hours, calming thoughts it does stir
When you roll on your back, chunky paws in the air
You command that I get up, and out of my chair!

Oh Kitty my love, you do captivate me
With your gold striking eyes through which life you do see,
With your chipmunk like cheeks, and your short stubby nose
I adore you my Kitty, from your ears to your toes

Oh Kitty my precious, you make my heart dance
As you play hide and seek
As you prowl and you prance
Entranced, I observe, as you scramble your tree
Bewitched by your temperament,
impulsive, care free

Oh Kitty, my Kitty, I worship you so,
You bring magic and mystery
I want all to know…
That a cat is unparalleled in joy that she brings
I'd choose Kitty over handbags and diamonds and rings

So my Kitty I thank you
For boosting my mood
When life is grey, black or murky
you feed me like food
Your medicinal displays of affection, though rare
My Kitty, you are somehow, for me, always there.

About The Author

Joy has always been a creative spirit. As a child, she filled her world with dance, music and writing – putting on impromptu performances and finding meaning in words far beyond her years. A deep thinker from the start, she carried this love of creativity into adulthood, weaving it into her life as a Mum, both sharing and writing poetry with her two children from the moment they were old enough.

A few years ago, she moved to a smallholding in Yorkshire. With sheep grazing in the fields and goats roaming the land, she got a sense of connection and calm she had never experienced before. Walking in the fresh air, witnessing the steady cycle of the seasons, and feeling the grounding presence of the animals around her.

Then came the diagnosis – stage 4 osteoporosis – and shortly after a terrible fall that forced her into stillness, leaving her unable to move as freely as before. Confined to her home, she found herself spending hours by the window, watching the land she had once walked so easily. At first, the quiet was frustrating. But in that stillness, something shifted. She returned to poetry, pouring her emotions onto the page, and in writing, she found healing.

Now, with her husband and three beloved cats by her side, she has rebuilt her life around the things that truly matter – family, movement, and peace. Through Yoga and Pilates, she has strengthened her body; through poetry and mindfulness, she has strengthened her spirit and mind. Her journey has been one of transformation, resilience, and deep reconnection – with herself, with nature, and with the quiet beauty of life as it is.

www.ingramcontent.com/pod-product-compliance
Lightning Source LLC
Chambersburg PA
CBHW041929040426
42444CB00019B/3474